Earth Science Explorers

BOOKWORMS

I0799347

LET'S EXPLORE EARTH'S ROCKS!

By Nicole Horning

Cavendish Square
New York

Published in 2021 by Cavendish Square Publishing, LLC
243 5th Avenue, Suite 136, New York, NY 10016

First Edition

Library of Congress Cataloging-in-Publication Data

Names: Horning, Nicole, author.
Title: Let's explore earth's rocks! / Nicole Horning.
Description: First edition. | New York : Cavendish Square Publishing, [2021] |
Series: Earth science explorers | Includes index.
Identifiers: LCCN 2019048462 (print) | LCCN 2019048463 (ebook) |
ISBN 9781502656230 (library binding) | ISBN 9781502656216 (paperback) |
ISBN 9781502656223 (set) | ISBN 9781502656247 (ebook)
Subjects: LCSH: Rocks–Juvenile literature.
Classification: LCC QE432.2 .H675 2021 (print) | LCC QE432.2 (ebook) |
DDC 552–dc23
LC record available at https://lccn.loc.gov/2019048462
LC ebook record available at https://lccn.loc.gov/2019048463

Editor: Nicole Horning
Copy Editor: Nathan Heidelberger
Designer: Rachel Rising

The photographs in this book are used by permission and through the courtesy of: Cover, DariaGa/Shutterstock.com; p. 5 Artography/Shutterstock.com; p. 7 Serg64/Shutterstock.com; p. 9 Ralf Lehmann/Shutterstock.com; p. 11 Zigzag Mountain Art/Shutterstock.com; p. 13 Darren J. Bradley/Shutterstock.com; p. 15 WiPhotoHunter/Shutterstock.com; p. 17 Leene/Shutterstock.com; p. 19 Richard Bradford/Shutterstock.com; p. 21 Sergejus Lamanosovas/Shutterstock.com; p. 23 Artur Bogacki/Shutterstock.com.

CPSIA compliance information: Batch #CS20CSQ: For further information contact Cavendish Square Publishing LLC, New York, New York, at 1-877-980-4450.

Printed in the United States of America

CONTENTS

Rocks Are Everywhere

Rocks are all around us. They take many years to form. Some rocks are softer than others. Some rocks are all one color, and other rocks are many colors. There are three types of rocks. Let's learn about them!

Igneous Rocks

Igneous rocks are made when hot, **melted** rock called magma cools. Magma comes from inside Earth. Sometimes magma cools under the gound. This forms one kind of igneous rock.

Sometimes magma cools above Earth's **surface**. Magma can come out through a hole in Earth's surface called a volcano. Then, it's called lava. When lava cools, it gets hard and forms another kind of igneous rock.

When lava cools quickly, the rocks that form are very smooth, or shiny. Sometimes they look like glass! Other kinds of igneous rock are rough, which means they're not smooth. These rocks have many **crystals**.

Sedimentary Rocks

Sedimentary rocks are made from pieces of other rocks. Sometimes a piece of a rock breaks away and is carried to another place. When pieces of rocks get pushed together, they form sedimentary rocks. The pieces can be very small or very big!

Sediment is matter at the bottom of a body of water. Sometimes pieces of sediment are carried by a river to a lake or ocean. When these pieces get pushed to the bottom of the water, they harden into a rock.

Sedimentary rocks have different sizes and shapes. Some have sharp parts. Others are smooth and round. Some sedimentary rocks look like they have stripes. This is because different kinds of sediment are pushed together over many years.

Metamorphic Rocks

Metamorphic rocks used to be igneous or sedimentary rocks. They were changed into metamorphic rocks because of heat and **pressure** deep in the ground. The heat makes the rocks change into another type of rock without melting them!

Because of how metamorphic rocks are changed, they may look squished or folded. These rocks may even look like they have stripes, or bands. This is because of how they were formed and other matter that was added to the rocks.

Rocks make up many of the objects people use every day. Pencils have rocks in them. Rocks can also be used to make roads and buildings. Rocks are very important!

WORDS TO KNOW

crystals: Small pieces of matter with many sides that harden to a clear form.

melted: Changed from solid to liquid with heat.

pressure: Force pushing on an object.

surface: The top part of something that can be seen.

INDEX